# YO-YO TRICKS

101 NEW TRICKS FOR YOUR YO-YO

JPV PUBLISHING

Third edition, 2019
ISBN: 978-1985145986
10 9 8 7 6 5 4 3 2 1

# CONTENTS

# INTRODUCTION

This book contains tips and tricks to ensure that you get the best and most exciting experience out of your yo-yo.

Having been around for centuries, the yo-yo is one of the most common toys in today's world.

So, **are you a new owner of a yo-yo**? Do you want to know more beyond just throwing the yo-yo? **Do you want to learn new tricks to impress your friends and family?**

If you answered "**YES**" to any of these questions, then **this book is for you**. This book contains multiple tips and tricks including which yo-yo to buy, how to maintain it and even how to make money from it! You just need to be ready to challenge yourself and your imagination.

The only challenge comes in with the learning curve involve and also the time investment required when starting out. However, this will all be worth it in no time.

However, at the same time, the yo-yo has managed to also become one of the most intriguing hobbies, one which has even been taken to professional stages through the World yo-yo contest held annually.

To help you get started, this book highlights twelve major chapters. You will cover the yo-yo 101 which gives a historical background of the yo-yo and how to compete professionally. You will also get to learn beginners', intermediate and finally, professional and expert yo-yo techniques.

This book also has a guide for buying your yo-yo, a guide on maintenance and finally, how to make money off your yo-yo.

These tips and tricks are definitely the best in the world today. Take time to practice and go through them. It will all be worth it in the end! Finally, remember that practice makes perfect.

Get ready to get started on your journey to becoming a yo-yo tricks professional and expert!

# ONE
## BEGINNER'S TRICKS

HAVE you just bought your first yo-yo or you are looking into getting your first yo-yo? Welcome! Owning a yo-yo is an exciting experience and the possibility of things you can do with the yo-yo makes it even better! In this chapter, we will look at some of the most suitable yo-yos for a starter and also some tricks to get you started on your journey!

**Choosing your First Yo-Yo**

Most people do not know or understand the different types of yo-yos available on the market and why it even matters. First of all, the type of yo-yo you have determine the types of tricks you can do and the ease of doing said tricks! When it comes to the selection, yo-yos can be defined based on a number of factors namely:

- **Shape**. There are different shapes such as the imperial yo-yo shape, modified yo-yo shape, and the butterfly shape. More modern styles include the v-shape, w-shape or stepped v, o-shape and the H-shaped.
- **Body**. This refers to material and structure of the yo-yo
- **String**. This refers to length and type of string used for the yo-yo. The different types of strings that exist include 100% cotton, 100% polyester, and cotton/polyester blend.

For a beginner, the recommended yo-yo is the Yomega Brain Yoyo or the Fizz Yoyo. These two yo-yos were specially designed for beginners to make learning the basics of using a yo-yo and doing tricks extremely easy and possible.

As explained above, the more advanced your tricks become, the more you will have to change the type of yo-yo you use.

With that, we can then have a look at some of the most common yo-yo tricks out there today.

## 1. The Sleeper

This is definitely the most common and most basic trick for beginners. In fact, the sleeper is the basis for all other throwing tricks. For this trick to be done, the yo-yo must be in the sleeping state or position.

This means remaining at the end of the uncoiled string while keeping the yo-yo spinning. In this sleeping position, the yo-yo can be used for tricks like 'rock the baby', 'walk the dog' and even 'around the world.'

The *sleeper trick* is where the yo-yo spins at the end of the string, this goes on for a significant period of time before going back to the hand.

Here is how you get started:

**Step One**: With your palm facing up, hold out your yo-yo. Ensure that your string is coming from the top-front of the yo-yo.

**Step Two**: Very swiftly, grab the yo-yo and flick it to the ground. The yo-yo should then remain on the ground, with the string end spinning.

**Step Three**: In this moment, turn your palm facing down. This will make the yo-yo spin for a while. Tug the yo-yo gently to bring it back to your hand!

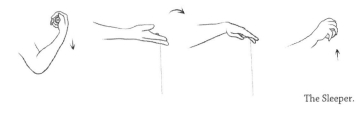

The Sleeper.

## 2. Walk the Dog

This is one of the most common tricks. It is more or less like walking a dog hence the name.

The gist of the trick is basically throwing a pretty strong sleeper then letting your yo-yo roll across the ground or floor right before you pull or tug it back to your hand.

To help you understand better, let us cover the trick in three basic steps:

**Step One**: Throw a fast sleeper. This is also referred to as 'taking your dog for a walk.'

**Step Two**: Next step is moving the yo-yo on the floor. Swing your yo-yo and gently set it on the ground all while letting it spin so that it moves on the floor.

**Step Three**: The last and final step is to bring the yo-yo back to your hand. You can do this by giving a slight tug and the yo-yo will come back to you!

Walk the dog.

**Tip**: *Avoid concrete surfaces like sidewalks for this trick since they can damage your yo-yo. The most suitable surfaces are carpets and rugs.*

### 3. The Elevator

This trick is one of the basic tricks and just requires you to have a strong sleeper. Understanding this trick will open doors to harder tricks like the brain twister.

To do this trick, here are the steps:

**Step One:** With your opposite hand between you and the string, push into the string.

**Step Two:** Lift your yo-yo up and place it on the string above your yo-yo finger.

**Step Three:** Then to make the yo-yo climb, pull your hands apart. This will make the yo-yo go up.

**Step Four:** Once up, toss the yo-yo up. This will make it spin then wind up and come right back to your hand!

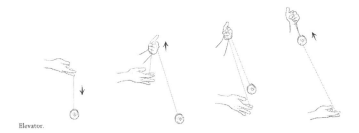

Elevator.

## How to String a Yo-Yo

This basically refers to changing an old string to a new string for your yo-yo. How do you do this?

**Step One:** Unwind the string completely so that there is nothing wound around the center of your yo-yo. Ensure that only the basic loop at the base is left.

**Step Two:** Holding the yo-yo with both hands, spin counter-clockwise to open up the yo-yo.

**Step Three:** Once inside, pull the string off the yo-yo.

**Step Four:** Put the new string on. Start by separating the loop with your fingers and tightening the string around the yo-yo before making the twists.

**Step Five:** Finally, you need to adjust and tighten your string. You can cut it to the desired length depending on your height and the tricks you wish to do.

## How to Wind a Yo-Yo

When it comes to how to wind a yo-yo, there are quite a few ways to do it. One common method is using your thumb to hold the string down on the inside edge of the yo-yo before you start winding.

This should be done for at least five windings before letting go. This method helps to prevent the yo-yo from spinning while winding.

We can also take a look at the different types of string that exist:

- **100% Cotton**. This type was more common decades ago. It has currently been replaced with pure polyester and other blends.
- **Pure Polyester**. This type of string is known to be stronger than cotton and even cotton/polyester blend. It is one of the most preferred by professionals due to its thinness and smooth feel.
- **Cotton/Polyester Blend** (50/50). This is one of the most versatile string types because of its strength and ease of use. This makes it perfect for use in any yo-yoing style. In case you are split on your purchase decision, then the 50/50 is your best bet.

# TWO

## GETTING YOUR YO-YO 101

IT IS safe to assume that you know what the Yo-yo is. In fact, we can also safely assume that you have played with or at least rolled a yo-yo once in your life.

Contrary to popular belief, these toys are not just meant for kids. In fact, with all the things that one can do with a yo-yo, it is safe to assume that yo-yos are actually more suited for adults.

If that isn't exciting news for you already, then gear up since in the next couple of chapters, we will look at yo-yos in depth, highlighting the different ways you can make your time more exciting with tricks and more tricks!

Before we embark into that, the yo-yo has been in existence for centuries now. In fact, the term or name yo-yo is believed to have originated from word 'yo yo' which is used to describe the swinging motion of the string attached to the yo-yo once it is released.

Let us help you to understand a bit of the origin of the yo-yo.

**A Little History behind the Yo-Yo**

To help you get a bit more perspective, let us look at the genesis of the yo-yo. This begs the question, where did yo-yos come from? According to historical sources, yo-yos have been in existence since the year 500BC.

Yo-yos were most common in ancient Greece and also in the Japanese culture. They were used by both children and adults as a pastime toy. Most at the time were made from wooden materials and pure cotton for the strings.

However, the birth of the modern yo-yo we know today was not until the 1920s. History brings up the name Pedro Flores. He is said to be the first man in history to open a yo-yo manufacturing factory which was located in Santa Barbara, California. He is also acknowledged as the man responsible for the redesign of the yo-yo into what we see and know today.

Noticing the potential of this fad industry, an investor called Donal F. Duncan purchased the company and the rest, as they say, is history! It was however not until 1932 that the name yo-yo was trademarked.

**Fun Facts about the Yo-Y o**

Yo-yos are so common in Japan such that the Japanese have won the World Yo-yo contest 71 times in the last 22 years!

- The first man to win the World Yo-yo contest was Harvey Lowe from London, England.
- The most prominent yo-yo player is Shinji Saito who has won the yo-yoing world title 13 times.
- The Duncan Toys Company yo-yo was inducted into the National Toy Hall of Fame in 1999. This was after the company opened their yo-yo factory in 1945.
- The youngest winner of the World Yo-Yo contest was an 11 year old in 2008.

**Why Should You Learn Tricks?**

First and foremost is to completely explore the full potential of the yo-yo. Why just roll when you can perform amazing tricks.

1. It is a great pastime activity for both exercise and productive playing.

2. You can get to compete professionally and win big!
3. You can make money performing your tricks for entertainment.
4. You get to impress people around you with your tricks
5. It is a great mind exercise since it improves your precision and moves since yo-yo tricks require you to be pretty fast!
6. Last but not least, it is fun! There is nothing as exciting as being able to perform some of the hardest yo-yo tricks.

# THREE
## INTERMEDIATE TRICKS

ONCE A BEGINNER MASTERS the easy yo-yo techniques, they will be able to learn the intermediate tricks. The easy design of the yo-yo makes it possible to perform quite a number of tricks.

With enough skill and coordination, you will be able to perform the following eleven intermediate yo-yo techniques. Perfect them by practicing these eleven easy moves repeatedly.

### 4. The Flying Saucer or Sleeping Beauty Trick

This amazing trick entails spinning the yo-yo while it is in midair, on its side, thus it resembles a spacecraft. This is more of a maintenance technique than a trick. It helps loosen or tighten the string. The string tightening techniques are easier for right-handed people.

**Step One**: While the yo-yo is held horizontally, throw it to the side at an angle. This will make the toy side spin as the string revolves around it loosely in the air.

**Step Two**: As it spins, grab the string with the left hand at about five or six inches from the yo-yo. The toy will resemble a flying saucer when you pull it up and out from the right to the left side.

**Step Three**: When the yo-yo slows down, wind it up by jerking it up with your left hand and use your right hand to pull it sideways. This will bring back the yo-yo to your right hand.

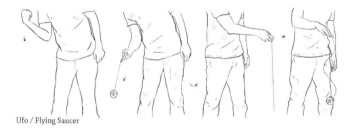

Ufo / Flying Saucer

## 5. The Loop Trick

This is one of the most complex tricks. It wholly depends on the movement of the wrist. Thus, make sure you practice it a couple of times with minimal arm movement.

**Step One**: Proceed by forward passing the yo-yo.

When it comes back, instead of catching it let it pass the inside of your arm.

**Step Two**: After this, snap the wrist in a circular motion, forward. This will send the yo-yo out again, and make it loop.

**Note**: *Take note that when making the loops maintain an outward arm position.*

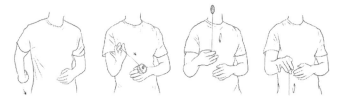

The Loop Trick

## 6. Hop the Fence Trick

**Step One**: The first step to this trick is throwing down the yo-yo.

**Step Two**: When it bounces back towards your hand, do not catch it.

**Step Three**: Let it hop past the top of your hand.

**Step Four**: Proceed by flicking your wrist and letting it move back down towards the ground.

**Step Five**: Continue the hopping stance. With some extra practice, you will be able to perfect this trick.

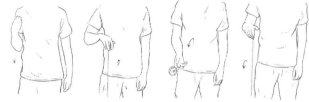

Hop the fence.

## 7. Dog Bite Trick

The secret to perfectly performing this trick is pretending that it accidentally happens. Prematurely announcing the "bite" might affect the trick.

**Step One**: Throw a fast sleeper to begin the trick.

**Step Two:** With feet about two feet apart, swing the yo-yo between them. Make sure that it swings below the knee.

**Step Three:** As this happens, jerk the string. This will make it "bite" your leg. It will brush against the inside of your pants as it comes back up.

Dog bite

**Tip**: *This will create a comical illusion, as you are required to act surprised by slowly turning around to search for it. As you search for it, the audience will find it comical that the yo-yo is stuck on the backside of your pants.*

## 8. Outside Loops Trick

This trick is similar to the Loop the loop trick. The difference between the two is that in the loop the loop trick, the yo-yo swings inside the wrist. On the other hand, the outside loops trick entails making the yo-yo swing outside the wrist.

**Step One:** Start by throwing the yo-yo forward. This is called a forward pass.

**Step Two:** As it bounces back, swing it past the top of your hand.

**Step Three:** Make sure that your palm is facing inward as you do this.

**Step Four:** Make the toy rotate your hand on the outside side of your wrist.

**Step Five:** Then, swing the toy forwards yet again by flicking your wrist.

**Step Six:** Maintain a low hand position. This is because a high positioned hand will make it very difficult to catch the yo-yo when it bounces back.

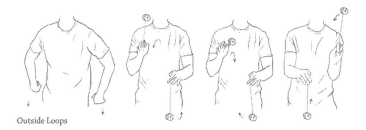

Outside Loops

## 9. Walk the Tightrope Trick

This technique helps you wind up the toy. It is more of a dare evil trick, thus most beginners do not really learn it at the beginning. This trick entails making the toy dangle at the knee.

**Step One:** Make sure that your yo-yo finger that holds the string is at the eye level position.

**Step Two:** Then, let go of it and allow it to dangle at the knee level.

**Step Three:** With the aid of your free hand, wrap the string around your forefinger.

**Step Four:** Use your yo-yo hand to grab it between the pinky finger and thumb at the knee level. You will notice that the string loop moves from the middle finger around the forefinger, straight to the yo-yo. The string that touches your middle finger should be below the toy.

**Step Five:** Proceed to drop the yo-yo gently on the string close to your yo-yo hand.

**Step Six:** Walk the yo-yo along that string by making it roll up. This trick is easier if the string is held firmly by the free hand. If you let that strong side over your finger, then it will not produce the required results.

**Step Seven:** When the toy reaches your free hand, hold it and wind it.

**Step Eight:** Wind it all the way up to the yo-yo hand. Alternatively, you could drop the yo-yo and proceed by winding it up similar to the way you would perform a gravity pull.

Walk the tightrope

## 10. Jump the Dog Through the Hoop

This trick is similar to the dog bite trick since they relate the yo-yo to a dog.

**Step One:** Start by assuming a similar position like you would when you walk the dog.

**Step Two:** However, instead of bringing the yo-yo in front of you, take it behind the leg.

**Step Three:** Swing the yo-yo on the same side of your yo-yo hand around the area beneath the leg.

**Step Four:** Place your yo-yo hand on the hip and form a hoop by arching your elbow away from your side.

**Step Five:** Bring the yo-yo back by jerking the string. If you opt to use a clutch yo-yo, you will have to wait for it to pull back automatically after engaging.

. . .

**Step Six:** Allow it to swing around your body and through the formed hoop.

Jump the dog through the hoop

## 11. Eiffel Tower Trick

**Step One:** With the aid of your free hand, open your forefinger and thumb.

**Step Two:** Position them about eight inches under the yo-yo.

**Step Three:** Then pull the yo-yo string upwards towards you.

**Step Four:** Use a counterclockwise motion with your yo-yo hand to bring your thumb towards the string.

**Step Five:** Form an "X" by rotating the string in a clockwise position. Use your free hand to achieve this position.

**Step Six:** Hold the string about eighteen inches from the toy.

**Step Seven:** Then pull it through the formed triangle and let it slide off out from your middle fingers and thumb.

**Step Eight:** Lastly, make the string go upwards through the loop. You released this same loop previously.

**Step Nine:** Then catch it with the hanging string between the ring finger and the yo-yo. This will display an Eiffel tower image.

EIFFEL TOWER

## 12. Corral Gate Trick or The Flag

This trick has unique string work.

**Step One:** Hold the yo-yo string about six inches from the yo-yo top. Do this with the aid of your first three fingers and pull it toward you. Take note that these are the fingers of your free hand.

**Step Two:** Use your yo-yo hand to reach down and hold the string. Also, do this with your first three fingers.

**Step Three:** Repeat this with your free hand.

**Step Four:** Complete the performance by using your pinky finger to reach over to the string and bringing it up to your fourth finger. This is the pinky finger of your yo-yo hand. This should result in an "X", which is referred to as the corral gate.

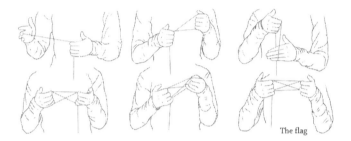

The flag

## 13. Monkey-Climb the Tree Trick

The yo-yo is viewed as the monkey in this trick.

**Step One:** Begin by pulling a fast sleeper.

**Step Two:** Then with the aid of your free hand, lift the yo-yo as it spins. Make sure that the yo-yo spins while it is above your hand.

**Step Three:** Position the string close to your yo-yo finger. Make sure that it is within the groove of your spinning yo-yo.

**Step Four:** Gently pull the yo-yo downward while

your free hand is still. This will make the toy look like it is "climbing" the string.

**Step Five:** When it reaches the top, slip it off the finger. This will make it wind up and go back to its initial position.

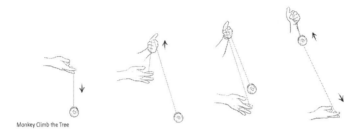

Monkey Climb the Tree

## 14. Thread the Needle Trick

This trick is similar to the monkey-climbing trick. The only difference is that its performance is horizontal as opposed to the vertical one of the climbing monkey trick.

**Step One:** Start by throwing fast sleeper. With the aid of your free hand, place your extended free hand under the string.

**Step Two:** Use it to lift the yo-yo upwards, similar to how you would perform the monkey-climbing trick.

**Step Three:** Make the string slip through the groove as the yo-yo sins, from behind.

**Step Four:** Then use the forefinger of your free hand and position it between the strings. Make sure that your free hand is upward and outward.

**Step Five:** Then pull backwards our yo-yo hand and walk the toy toward your free hand. Do this, while maintaining the toy along the string.

**Step Six:** As the toy approaches the forefinger, slip the finger outside the loop.

**Step Seven:** Then jerk the string to make it wind up.

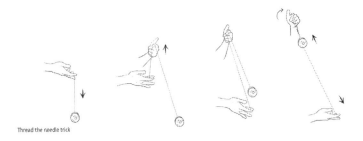

Thread the needle trick

# FOUR

# TRICKS TO IMPRESS YOUR FAMILY AND FRIENDS

TO BECOME A PROFESSIONAL YO-YO PLAYER, you have to start with the easy tricks before you learn the unique and complex ones. These tricks can be mastered within a short period. Thus, these basic stunts will come in handy when you want to impress your loved ones during occasions.

They are easy to learn, thus you can pull them off after having an impromptu lesson. Even though they are easy to learn, make sure you still practice to perfect them. Do not shy away from trying again after failing at the first instance.

## 15. Gravity Pull Trick

**Step One:** This is the classic trick. It is the first trick that comes to mind when most people hear the term "yo-yo"

**Step Two:** Grab the toy and put some distance between you and it. Make sure that your palms are facing downward as you try out this technique.

**Step Three:** Open your yo-yo hand and allow it to drop toward the ground.

**Step Four:** When the toy reaches the end of the string, jerk it up firmly.

**Step Five:** This will wind it up and pull it back to your hand. This is the easiest trick of them all.

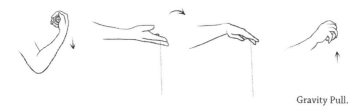

Gravity Pull.

## 16. Throw Down Trick

**Step One:** Most of the complex yo-yo techniques begin with this simple trick.

**Step Two:** Position your hand out in front of you, with your palm facing upwards.

**Step Three:** Place the yo-yo on the edge of the palm with the aid of the middle finger and thumb.

**Step Four:** Make sure that the palm is in line with your shoulder to perform this trick effectively.

**Step Five:** Allow the yo-yo to flow out in front of you as your string curls up over the top of the toy.

**Step Six:** Proceed to flick your wrist. This will send the yo-yo to the ground firmly. Make sure that the yo-yo goes straight down and not lean on any other side.

**Step Seven:** When the toy exhausts its string, tug at it slightly to pull it back into position.

## 17. The Sleeper

This trick is similar to the gravity pull in an up-and-down mode. Most people prefer to learn it after learning the gravity pull and throw down tricks. Most of the yo-yo tricks incorporate this trick at the beginning. Learning the sleeper trick, will open doors for a better understanding of the other complex tricks.

**Step One:** It starts out just the same as the thrown down trick.

**Step Two:** Hold the toy outward, while your palm faces upwards. Make sure that the string comes off at the front and top of the toy. The same way that you throw a fastball is the same way you will proceed to throw the yo-yo.

**Step Three:** Hold it and flick it sharply and firmly towards the ground. The toy should maintain a spinning position at the end of the string.

**Step Four:** As it spins, make your yo-yo hand palm face down. With the right tension, the toy should keep spinning at the end for a while.

**Step Five:** Then complete the trick by jerking the string and allowing it to wind back up to its original position.

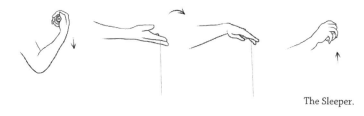

The Sleeper.

## 18. Reverse Sleeper

Just as the name suggests this trick is similar to the sleeper tick. However, the yo-yo tends to spin back when it is thrown downwards.

**Step One:** With hand extended, place the yo-yo in its edge. To perform this, your palm has to be facing upwards so it is when doing the sleeper trick.

**Step Two:** With the yo-yo between your middle finger and thumb, make the string flow out of the yo-yo from its bottom back. This is what differentiates the sleeper from the reverse sleeper.

**Step Three:** Flick your wrist to firmly whip the yo-yo to the ground.

**Step Four:** Throw it downwards and make sure it does not lie on any other side as you do this. This will throw the yo-yo back when you throw it down.

**Step Five:** Jerk the string to return the yo-yo to its original position.

## 19. Pinwheel Trick

This is a very unique and beautiful trick that would serve well in a performance before your loved ones.

**Step One**: Start by throwing a fast sleeper.

**Step Two:** Hold the string with the free hand middle finger and thumb. Do this at about two-thirds of the string as the yo-yo flows down.

**Step Three:** Shift your free hand to the side, upwards. Make sure that it is away from the rest of your body and move the yo-yo hand downwards. This will make the yo-yo maintain a swinging position, swing it in circles.

**Step Four:** Make about four or more pinwheel-turns and make the final turn different. Do this by throwing the toy upwards and forward.

**Step Five:** Release the string after doing this and use your yo-yo hand to catch the yo-yo.

*Tip:* *Make sure that the palm is facing upwards to perform this stance effectively*

## 20. Walk the Cat Trick

This rib-cracking trick is definitely one to learn in preparation for a rainy day. The entire routine is based on the idea that cats are very stubborn. They never do what you want them to.

**Step One**: Start by throwing a reverse sleeper.

**Step Two**: Slowly walk forward and make the toy touch the ground. The yo-yo will walk behind you since it is spinning back.

**Step Three**: As the toy exhausts the walking area and reaches the end, allow it to jerk it backwards. As if, the cat is pulling you off balance.

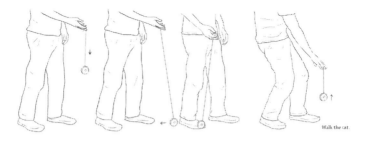

Walk the cat.

*Tip: Make it comical by acting surprised and letting the toy jerk your entire body behind as well.*

## 21. Forward Pass Trick

You will definitely wow the crowd with this trick.

**Step One**: Take the yo-yo and hold it as though you are performing the throw does trick.

**Step Two**: However, instead of putting your yo-yo hand upwards, as you would on a throw down trick, take it to the side.

**Step Three**: Turn it and make the back of the hand face forward. Swing your arm and wrist forward. This will throw the toy in front directly.

**Step Four**: When it exhausts the trying, tug it slightly and turn your hand over.

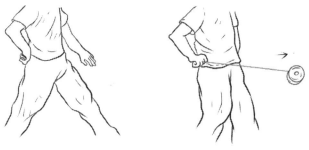

Forward pass trick

*Tip*: *When you turn your hand over, your palm will face your upwards and allow you to catch the toy.*

## 22. Around the World Trick

This beautiful and easy trick incorporates both the forward pass and the sleeper.

**Step One**: Start by pulling a forward pass with the yo-yo.

**Step Two**: When the yo-yo exhausts the string, jerk it back and swing it over the yo-yo shoulder.

**Step Three**: Let it pass behind your back to take a complete 360-degree arc. Make sure that the yo-yo maintains the ending position throughout the routine.

**Step Four**: When the toy rotates and gets back to the initial point, jerk it back.

**Step Five**: Since this technique requires the toy to rotate, make sure that you are conscious of your surroundings.

**Step Six**: Make sure that as it rotates it does not hit your audience or the surrounding items.

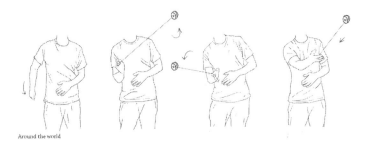

Around the world

*Tip: If you will perform it indoors, make sure that the room has high ceilings and open spaces. Performing in a cramped up room with low ceilings will not only affect the performance but it will also affect the surrounding items.*

## 23. Around the Corner Trick

This trick is also known as the orbit launch trick.

**Step One**: Kick it off with a hard sleeper trick.

**Step Two**: Swing the yo-yo string behind and around the upper part of the yo-yo arm. This will make the toy hang behind you. It will drape over the upper part of your arm slightly above the elbow.

**Step Three**: Hold the string using your yo-yo hand, spin it with your index finger, and thumb.

**Step Four**: Once this is one, jerk the toy up and let it wind up as it goes past the top of your arm.

**Step Five**: Allow the yo-yo to continue to the floor, and then push it back to its initial position as you would in a gravity pull trick.

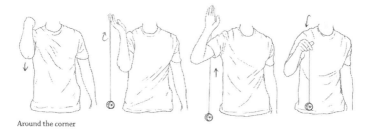

Around the corner

*Tip: Make sure the yo-yo is spinning swiftly before you tag at the string.*

## 24. Breakaway Trick

This yo-yo trick is a spectacle to behold because it seems to defy the laws of gravity. For a small second, the yo-yo will appear to be hanging in mid-air.

**Step One**: Place the toy on your hand and bend your hand as you would when you flex your muscle.

**Step Two**: Proceed by releasing the yo-yo when you

swing your arm. The yo-yo will fly downwards and out, when you bring it down. Right-handed players need to swing their arms towards the left in an arc, across the front of the body.

**Step Three**: Let the toy swing out to the opposite side of the body in front of you.

**Step Four**: Make it hand in mid-air for a while, then jerk the string to take it back to its initial position.

The breakaway

## 25. Three-Leaf Clover Trick

This trick coins its name from the movement that the yo-yo makes. The movement seems to take the shape of a three-leaf clover.

**Step One**: Throw a vertical loop over your head to start.

**Step Two**: As it comes back, send the yo-yo outwards right in front of you. This will resemble the movement you make when throwing a forward pass.

**Step Three**: As the yo-yo bounces back, send it out the third time in the direction of the ground. This is similar to the movement made when making the throw down trick.

**Step Five**: Catch the toy when it comes back this time to complete the cycle.

Three-leaf clover trick

# FIVE

## LOOPING TRICKS

HERE WE WILL GET into the basics of looping if you are now ready to learn something new. Looping tricks are *best done with a round shaped yo-yo* which typically has a tighter gap so that the string can grab it accordingly and shoot it out very fast.

This also provides more control for when you are throwing the yo-yo. Looping involves throwing out the yo-yo repeatedly while controlling its movement. This mode of yo-yoing is one of the more conventional styles that people have been performing for years now.

Now that we know what looping is, you want to make sure the yo-yo string gets onto your hand in the proper manner because there is a skill to it.

**Step One**: Make sure you have a good slipknot in

place, as this is a crucial part of looping because it prevents the loop from shooting off your hand so that you do not lose control of the yo-yo.

**Step Two**: Place the slipknot around your hand so that one side has a double strand and the other side has a single strand. The double-stranded side should face away from you and not towards the throwing hand.

If this was not so, as you are looping, the yo-yo comes back around and due to the manner in which the slip-knot grabs, it is simply going to swing around and as the person is looping it, it makes it harder to control the yo-yo string when it is spinning continually around the finger.

When bringing the string over while tightening it as you are attempting to perform loops, it will not move anywhere, as the slipknot will be pulling it tighter with every loop performed.

It will remain stationary and this is what will help in controlling the loops better. Once you are sure of where the two-handed strings are supposed to be then you will be prepared to learn some looping tricks.

### Adjusting the Yo-yo Strings for the Looping Tricks

Your yo-yo needs to be set up in a different way

compared to how it was set up for most of the **1A tricks**.

When opening your looping yo-yo, the gap is very tight, which is a crucial element. The yo-yo's gap should be very close so that it can grab the string easily. You will have two O-rings with certain yo-yos on either side, which is what will be used for response, and what will make the yo-yo shoot back.

There is also a small bearing on the inside. For such yo-yos, it is advisable to use one with a clean bearing inside and a very tight gap to help the user control the yo-yo.

Another essential element to looping is the length of the string. A longer string affords you less control when performing a loop while a shorter string gives you more control.

A recommended length would be from just about your pocket all the way down. Cut it at about your pocket and tie the loop then you will be all set. You can experiment with varying string lengths and find out what works best for you.

### 26. Forward Pass

This is the first looping trick you should learn and it includes throwing the yo-yo out and catching it.

**Step One**: For this trick, however, it is crucial that you throw the yo-yo to the very end of the string and make sure you have a nice strong throw.

**Step Two**: Speed your forward pass up slightly allowing you to control the yo-yo right out and then back in. Looping yo-yos swing back a lot faster because they have a tighter gap.

**Step Three**: Ensure you get a nice straight and strong throw while aiming in such a way that you can see the yo-yo shooting out directly.

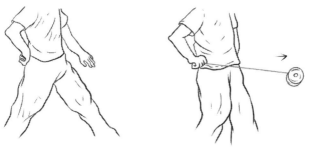

Forward pass trick

## 27. Around the World

**Step One**: For this move, shoot the yo-yo around and it will come back for the catch.

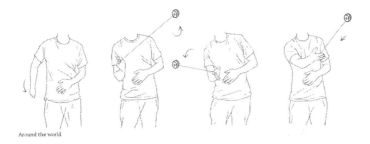

Around the world

*Tip:* You need to perform this move strong and fast and when you are starting out it is alright if the yo-yo is almost coming around and almost shooting back on you.

## 28. The Tidal Wave

**Step One**: This model begins with a throw and then you will swing out the yo-yo. It is almost half of a real loop because you are swinging it out to get that loop motion.

**Step Two**: Ensure you throw out a strong sleeper by taking your non-throwing end and bring it up to the string the swing out the yo-yo up in front of you. You want your hand to be slightly closer to the yo-yo allowing you to bring it up straight and then release it.

**Step Three**: So one more time the movement includes throwing out the yo-yo back out, bring it up and swing it. Then throw it out once again.

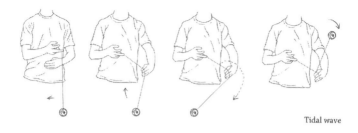

## 29. A Basic Loop

**<u>Step One</u>**: For this motion, you will throw the yo-yo out once it comes back around and your hand will come back in almost to the point where you would typically throw it and shoot it right back out. You will be doing that repeatedly.

The Loop Trick

## 30. Outside Loops

This is the next trick to learn once you know how to do a basic loop.

**<u>Step One</u>**: Outside loops involve you throwing the yo-yo outside of your wrist instead of inside. The yo-yo will come around at the back of your hand and will not go inside the arm.

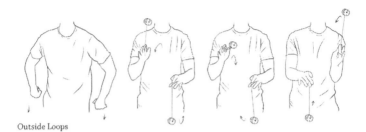

Outside Loops

## 31. Hop the Fence

This type of looping trick is not usually thrown like a conventional loop as it actually comes down.

You will throw the yo-yo, it will come down repetitively over your hand, and you will be controlling the yo-yo down to the end of the string.

**Step One**: Start by throwing the yo-yo slightly sideways and you will find that it is at a slight angle and when you want to throw it back again, it will be easier to come over right over the top of your hand.

**Step Two**: When you throw it slightly sideways, you will be able to control it repeatedly.

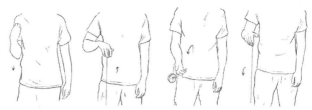

Hop the fence.

# SIX

# EXPERT YO-YO TRICKS

THESE ARE tricks that are guaranteed to amaze the crowd with examples such as Spirit Bomb, Suicide, and Revolutions in any freestyle performance.

## 32. Suicide

In this trick, you will fling the yo-yo string around and catch the loop. On the other hand, Suicide 1.5 is quite similar except that the user catches the loop with their throw hand as opposed to their non-throwing hand. The user catches the loop as it comes over.

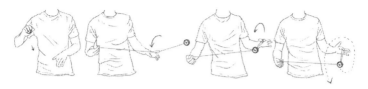

The suicide

## 33. Skinning the Gerbil

This one cool trick is worth the extra effort. If you manage to get it down smooth and fast, you can be sure that you will be able to impress many people. It is quite smooth and when you are performing it, it flows really well. The trick moves back and forth hitting all the sides of the yo-yo string.

**Step One**: Start by landing on a trapeze; take your throwing hand and turn it inward toward yourself then push in on the hair of the string. This enables it to string around further as you push in with your throwing hand without the string knotting up.

**Step Two**: Next, you will go around and land it two times onto the string.

**Step Three**: Double up on the yo-yo string to make sure it comes back around twice.

**Step Four**: Afterwards, you will push, in, then double

up, come around, and land it on the other side of the string.

**Step Five**: Next, we have the second part of this smooth flowing trick. When skinning the gerbil, get your ears spinning very fat, make it smooth, and ensure it is dead center on the yo-yo string.

**Step Six**: The next step involves missing the string completely, then coming around and hitting the string.

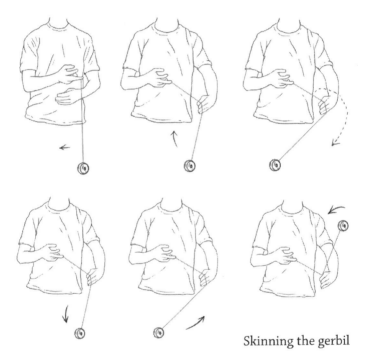

Skinning the gerbil

## 34. Revolutions

This is a slack string trick and it is performed when the string is pinched and whipped around in mid-air then back into a catch. It is a great stage trick and looks very fancy so people really get into it.

**Step One**: Pinch the string between the pointer finger of your throwing hand and your thumb while starting the yo-yo back up again.

**Step Two**: From this motion, it has to be one smooth motion and once it hits, you will pinch and allow the string to fall over.

**Step Three**: The loop is what will be flying around there so that you will be taking the yo-yo and swinging it on the outside and the inside repeatedly. Try the movement dead to get a feel of it and make sure you end on the inside while replacing your finger.

**Step Four**: Pinch and swing in one smooth motion outside and inside as many times as you would like and bring it inside as you finish then switch to your pointer finger replacing it in the string.

1

2

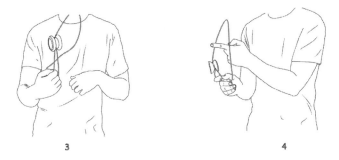

3

4

Revolutions


## 35. The Wrist Mount

**Step One**: This trick begins with the user going over their fingers as if they were going to perform a trapeze but instead they will continue the yo-yo over and stick their wrist out almost as though they were in a double or nothing. You want to ensure that it is going over your wrist. It should go over the back of the user's wrist to ensure that it is lined up.

**Step Two**: As the yo-yo comes around, the user takes his or her hand and twists it.

**Step Three**: The user puts their thumb opening up the triangle forming.

**Step Four**: As the string is coming underneath, it will land on the string it is connected to-the string coming under the user's wrist and then land it straight into the middle.

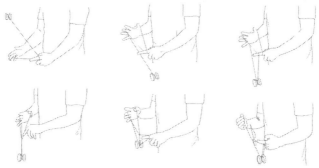

Wrist mount

## 36. Spirit Bomb

Follow the steps to give it a try:

**Step One**: Start with the wrist mount.

**Step Two**: Try creating the loop around your wrist, as shown in the illustration.

**Step Three**: Roll under the yoyo, instead of twisting

your hand. You are going to roll your yoyo under those two strings in the photo. Once you get the rhythm, you will see the yoyo is rolling at itself, without you putting much effort.

**Step Four**: Toss the yoyo up while it is rolling. You will notice a bit of triangle up there, with a string below it. Land the yoyo on that string.

**Step Five**: Roll back, and twist your hand. While you roll back, the string will be at your closest distance. You can now quickly get the yoyo back to your hand.

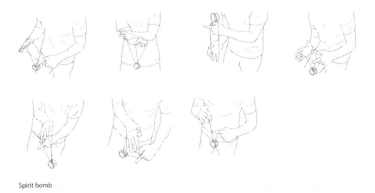

Spirit bomb

***Note***: The trickiest part is the step three where you have to uncross your hand from the two strings. So practicing more will make you an expert.

## 37. Double Suicide

Before you embark on this cool trick, you should make sure you can perform suicide first.

**Step One**: The loop is thrown over and the loop created is caught repeatedly.

**Step Two**: For the double suicide, the user will be hitting their yo-yo on the string making an extra loop to sort of fly around.

It comes back around twice while shooting around very fast this means that you need to catch it very fast.

**Step Three**: Double on and when it is coming back around twice you will catch it with your fingers.

*Tip:* *One way to make it easier to catch while coming around on the string is to push down further. This move is very hard and you might not be able to make it work anytime you try doing it.*

# SEVEN

# TWO-HANDED YO-YO TRICKS

THIS CATEGORY of tricks might come across as difficult to learn, but they are definitely amazing to look at. After moving from the expert level, you are now ready to perform with a yo-yo in both hands keeping in mind that practice is crucial and patience is essential.

2A tricks involve two-handed yo-yoing and looping tricks and you will need a lot of time to master them. These tricks are centered on the loop, around the world, and the forward pass so you might want to make sure you are proficient in these basic moves as the 2A tricks are simply variations of the above mentioned tricks.

The loop involves throwing out the yo-yo and

swinging it repeatedly back out in the air. If you practice this trick enough times you will be able to perform it with two hands. It is known as double A (2A) or two-handed yo-yoing.

## 38. Sidewinder

**Step One**: Throw while moving your hand to the side for the string to ravel around the yo-yo which in turn tightens and loosens the string based on the direction in which you want it to go.

This is a crucial trick in double-A yo-yoing because whenever you perform a loop, the yo-yo ends up loosening the string as it turns around. Doing this continually would mean that the yo-yo would end up flying off the string eventually.

If you are performing this move with your left hand, the movement will only tighten the string so much so that it will bind up and will not be able to come out.

*Tip:* The sidewinder trick allows you to tighten and loosen *the string so you can control the string tension with different moves as well.*

## 39. Punching Bags

This is one of the harder Double-A tricks and it is dependent on the hop off the fence trick so ensure you are familiar with that move.

The yo-yo essentially goes down over the user's hand repetitively. For the punching bags trick, you will have extreme movement with both hands almost as though you are punching.

**Step One**: Begin with a hop the fence and learn to eventually shoot it up to develop the punching motion.

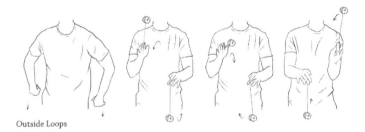

Outside Loops

*Tip: The yo-yo should be above the shoulder slightly to give you optimum control.*

. . .

## 40. Ride the Horse

This trick makes for great practice and it helps the brain work on getting both the hands to work at once.

**Step One**: The trick works by performing a hop the fence with one hand and looping with the other. The horse riding motion is almost evident as you perform the trick.

## 41. Shoot the Moon + Loops

**Step One**: Practice on gaining strength-performing loops with one hand and shooting the moon with the other hand.

**Step Two**: Perform the looping trick with your normal hand and simultaneously perform the shoot the moon move with the other hand.

Some people find it easier doing the shoot the moon using their dominant hand enabling them to hold more control over the trick.

## 42. Vertical Punches

These are also known as vertical loops and comprise of two-handed vertical movement of the yo-yo mid-air.

**Step One**: You have the option of beginning with the

shoot the moon trick bringing it up and shooting them directly in mid-air.

*Tip: Perform the motion with both hands. The trick to this move is to make sure the yo-yo is at the very end of the string while getting in a strong throw to help the yo-yo remain in the air.*

EIGHT

# WORLD YO-YO CONTEST

IF YOU ARE new to professional yo-yoing, I bet you did not know that yo-yo competitions exist! Well, they have existed for decades now, the biggest and most competitive one being the world yo-yo competition.

This annual yo-yo festival was started by yoyoguy.com in Florida and has over the years moved to other nations such as Czech Republic, Japan, Iceland, Poland, UK and even China. Today, it even incorporates players from over 5 continents!

If that is too much for you, then maybe you can organize a smaller yo-yo competition in your locality or school. Here are some basics to get you going:

When it comes to a standard yo-yo competition, there are normally two sections: the compulsory tricks and the freestyle.

- **Compulsory Tricks**. This is also known as a trick ladder. These are pre-selected tricks chosen prior to the contest which a player must complete successfully either on their first or second attempt.
- **Freestyle**. This is where a competitor does a personal routine to some music before a judging panel. Here, the distinguishing factors are artistic performance, synchronization with the music playing and finally, the difficulty of

the tricks being performed. These are usually about 3 minutes long.

When it comes to contest divisions, most yo-yo competitions range as follows: 1A, 2A, 3A, 4A, 5A, and AP.

**1A** involves a player performing tricks that manipulate the string using a long sleeping yo-yo. Normally this is held as the last event due to its popularity.

**2A** involves a player playing around with two yo-yo s to do looping tricks. This is probably the most visually exciting events!

**3A** involves tricks that manipulate the string but this time around with two yo-yos with long strings each tied to its own hand.

**4A** is probably one of the more challenging acts. It involves using an off string yo-yo that is released into the air and the player has to attempt to catch it with an artistic flare.

**5A** unlike most tricks does not involve tying the yo-yo to a finger but instead using a counterweight.

**AP**. This stands for artistic performance. Here, a player becomes a performer and can use props and different types of yo-yos to do a freestyle show.

With this information, you are now ready to embark on your journey as a professional yo-yoer. You can also use this criteria to plan small contest between you and your friends or family.

**Yo-Yo Contest**

The World Yo-Yo Contest is the culminating yo-yo competition of the worldwide competitive circuit and is considered the most prestigious yo-yo competition in the world.

The winner of this competition in any of the six championship divisions is deemed the World Yo-Yo Champion—the only event to award such a title. The contest attracts competitors from all over the world, and an increasingly large number of spectators.

The competition is currently run by the International Yo-Yo Federation (IYYF) and the respective host nation's national organization. As of 2015, 33 countriesha ve fed into the World Yo-Yo Contest from their respective national yo-yo contests. The 2016 contest was held on August 3–6 in the city of Cleveland

**Location**

Following the creation of the IYYF in 2013, The

World Yo-Yo Contest now cycles between America, Europe, and Asia.

This cycling is scheduled through 2018. The bidding process involves the IYYF and the interested National Organization. After finals of the 2016 WYYC on day 4, Steve Brown announced a bid for the 2018 WYYC in Shanghai, China.

- 2014 Europe (Prague, Czech Republic)

- 2015 Asia (Tokyo, Japan)

- 2016 United States of America (Cleveland, Ohio)

- 2017 Europe (Reykjavik, Iceland)

- 2018 Asia (Shanghai, China)

- 2019 United States of America (Cleveland, Ohio)

**Winners by Country & Players**

The World Yo-Yo Contest has historically been dominated by the Japanese-taking home 71 World Titles in the past 22 years The United States has also had a lesser dominance, taking home 26 World Titles.

Shinji Saito remains the most decorated yo-yoer of all-time with 13 World Titles. Takeshi Matsuura is second with 7.

In 2003, Brazil's Rafael Matsunaga became the first

player outside Japan or the United States to win a World Title, doing so in 5A (Counterweight).

In 2004, Hiroyuki Suzuki won his first World Title. Both Daisuke Shimada and Shinji Saito won their third World Title in as many years.

Hiroyuki Suzuki became the first player to ever win back-to-back titles in the 1A division in 2005. Shinji Saito continued his dominance, winning his fourth World Title in the 2A division.

Kentaro Kimura won the 3A division with what is considered the greatest 3A routine of all time in 2009.

In 2010, Canada's Jensen Kimmitt became the first player outside Japan or the United States to win a World Title in 1A. Without Shinji Saito entering the 2A division, Yashushi Furakawa won the World Title. Singapore's Marcus Koh became the second player outside of the United States or Japan to win in the 1A division. Shinji Saito also returned from a year competition hiatus to win the 2A division for a record eighth time.

In 2012, Switzerland's inmot!on became the first team outside Japan or the United States to win the Artistic Performance (AP) division. It was also the first ever World Title won by European competitors.

In 2013, Hungary's Janos Karancz became the first European to win the 1A division at the World Yo-Yo Contest. 2013 was also the first, and only, year to feature a top-3 in 1A with no players from Japan or the United States.

In 2014, Rei Iwakura completed a flawless routine in the 4A division en route to his third World Title.

## Championship Division Structure

There are a series of preliminary rounds before the final round at the World Yo-Yo Contest. In the past, anyone could enter the World Yo-Yo Contest. Competitors were allowed a one-minute routine, and a set number of players would make the finals. The preliminary rounds have been evolving over the years to accommodate the growing popularity of competitive yo-yos around the world.

## Sanctioned Seeding Competitions

Players can earn a seed to various rounds of the preliminaries through Multi-National Competitions, National Competitions, and the previous year's World Yo-Yo Contest.

1. European Yo-Yo Championship (Kraków, Poland)

2. Las Vegas Yo-Yo Championship (Las Vegas, United States)

3. Asia Pacific Yo-Yo Championship (Singapore, Singapore)

4. Latin American Yo-Yo Championship (Mexico City, Mexico)

5. Previous year's World Yo-Yo Contest (Prague, Czech Republic)

6. One of 33 IYYF approved National Competitions

**Non-Championship Divisions**

In addition to these World Divisions, the World Yo-Yo Contest also hosts several non-championship divisions such as the 'Women's Freestyle' and, in 2015, the 'Over 40 Freestyle. There is also numerous yo-yo modifying and design contests, known in the field as modding. These non-championships divisions do not award the title of 'World Yo-Yo Champion'.

**Articipating Nations**

There are 33 countries currently registered [7] with the IYYF that have the right to seed a National Champion into the semi-final round at the World Yo-Yo Contest. IYYF is also in communication with several other countries [8] (denoted by *), but, currently, these countries do not have the right to seed a National Champion to the semi-finals.

## How To Run A Yo-Yo Contest

If you have ever organized a contest, my hat is off to you. It's not an easy thing. Even the smallest local contest organizer has a lot of responsibility. It's not a thankless job, the people that attend are always very appreciative, but as far as recognition outside of that, not much is done.

Having said that, this article isn't about complaining, it's about giving you a realistic outline of what goes into running a contest. Who knows, you might actually want to run one after reading this! At the very least you might look at approaching the local contest organizer and offering to help out.

For anyone who has attended a contest, you know there are some things to expect. You can generally expect qualified judges and a stage. You can expect to see vendor tables to shop at, a practice area and somewhere to sit.

There's a sound system for the music and nowadays there is an expectation of a live stream, or at least high quality video is posted to youtube afterward.

There are prizes, often a raffle. A good contest usually has access to food and drink as well. You also might notice the banner with the sponsor's logos on it.

Generally this is all put together a handful of people, headed up by a single person.

## Rules & Regulations

General Freestyle Rules for Championship Divisions

General Rules and Guidelines – All Styles

## Time

Time starts between 0:00 and 0:01 on the music, and ends between 1:00 and 1:01, 2:00 and 2:01.

Prelim freestyles will be 1-minute long. Finals freestyles will be 2 minutes long.

## Start

Yo-Yo(s) may not start the freestyle from a spinning, thrown, or mounted.

## Finish

No points score after the end time of the performance, deductions may still be taken.

## Music

Each competitor shall have 2-minutes to perform a freestyle routine to his or her choice of music for the freestyle finals, and 1-minute for the prelims.

The 2-minute (or 1-minute) time period starts when the music is started by the sound manager.

No points shall be scored for either Technical Execution or Performance Style for any reason before the music starts, or after the 2-minutes (or 1-minute time period) have elapsed.

Music shall start from the beginning of the track and shall be played for 2-minutes (1-minute during prelims) where it shall be cut off. Contestants can feel free to edit the music so that it fades out or ends at the appropriate time.

Music that terminates prior to the 2 minute (or 1-minute) time period will be considered to end the freestyle performance unless the competitor notifies the sound manager and contest director prior to the freestyle so the judges may be informed.

All music must be considered G-rated (appropriate for all audiences) and shall not contain offensive lyrics including but not limited to: obscenities, ethnic or sexual slurs, violence advocacy, etc.

If you are unsure about your music, a judge will be available to listen to your music and make sure it is appropriate. Music used in many video games, television segments, and other media does not necessarily meet this standard. With the concurrence of the Contest Director and the Head Judge, use of inappropriate music by a competitor shall result in their disqualification.

**Stage Use**

All actions of a competitor must be G-rated (appropriate for all audiences) and take into account the safety of the audience, facility, and the competitor. With the concurrence of the Contest Director and the Head Judge, dangerous or inappropriate behavior by a competitor shall result in their disqualification.

No assistants are allowed on stage while a competitor is performing. All extra yo-yos that are to be used by a competitor shall be ready to use and must be brought on stage, before their freestyle starts on a tray supplied by the Contest.

Yo-yos that leave the stage during a freestyle shall not be returned to the stage and no others shall be accepted by the competitor from the audience or an assistant.

If a competitor uses a yo-yo in violation of this rule, the judges will not award any points for Technical Execution or Performance Style while that yo-yo is in play, but shall deduct points for any mistakes, loss of control restarts, yo-yo replacements, etc.

No props are allowed on stage or to be used in the competition without the prior approval of the Contest Director and the Head Judge. Hats and glasses are excepted and do not require approval as long as they are not significantly altered. All reasonable request for props will be considered if they are presented prior to the start of the competition.

Yo-Yos with hub stacks (or similar outside mounted bearings) or rim bearings are allowed in all divisions.

**Division Specific Rules**

Specific Considerations for 1A Freestyles

In a 1A freestyle, at no time shall there be more than one yo-yo in play (including slave or prop yo-yos) at the same time.

During any periods of time that this rule is violated, the judges shall not grant any points for Technical Execution or Performance Style but shall deduct points for any mistakes, loss of control restarts, yo-yo replacements, etc.

In a 1A freestyle, (except for the "Mobius style and Skyrocket type tricks provisions below") at no time shall the yo-yo be removed from the string (i.e. no offstring tricks are allowed). During any periods of time that this rule is violated, the judges shall not grant any points for Technical Execution or Performance Style but shall deduct points for any mistakes, loss of control restarts, yo-yo replacements, etc.

In a 1A freestyle, Mobius style is allowed. Skyrocket type tricks are also allowed. In a 1A freestyle, typical scoring elements include but are not limited to: mounts, dismounts, string hits, hops, grinds, lacerations, release catches (like suicides/Iron Whips), slack catches, regenerations and binds.

## Specific Considerations for 2A and 3A Freestyles

In a 2A or 3A freestyle, the judges shall not grant any points for Technical Execution or Performance Style unless both yo-yos are in play simultaneously. In a 2A or 3A freestyle, at no time shall there be more than two yo-yos in play (including slave or prop yo-yos) at the same time.

During any periods of time that this rule is violated, the judges shall not grant any points for Technical Execution or Performance Style but shall deduct points for any mistakes, loss of control restarts, yo-yo replacements, etc. In a 2A freestyle, typical scoring elements include but are not limited to: loops, punches, wraps, tanglers, moons, hops, stalls, worlds, transitions, regenerations and various combinations and/or variations of these elements.

In a 3A freestyle, typical scoring elements include but are not limited to: 1A type string tricks that involve both yo-yo's simultaneously, however transitions between tricks may involve tanglers, worlds, grinds, wraps and similar elements.

## Specific Considerations for 4A and 5A Freestyles

In a 4A and 5A freestyle there is no restriction on the number of yo-yos that may be in play at the same time. In a 4A freestyle, typical scoring elements include but are not limited to: launches, tosses, catches, regenerations, grinds, intentional bounces off body parts or the stage back to a catch, boingys or other types of bounces between strings.

In a 4A freestyle, trick elements performed with a pinched string that mimic 1A trick elements, where the yo-yo never leaves the string for the entire duration of the trick element, may be scored at a lower value than high risk off string moves. Similarly, 4A railing style tricks (sliding along the string) may be scored at a lower value than high risk off string moves.

In a 5A freestyle, points shall only be awarded only while the counter weight (or multiple counter weights) is in play, or in the act of being moved from hand to hand. Any trick done while the counterweight is being held for the entire duration of the trick shall be considered 1A trick, and shall not be scored.

**Preliminary Freestyle Scoring:**

• Technical Execution: 60% (clicker, normalized)

• Technical Evaluation: 20% (Cleanliness and Execution – 0 to 10 points each)

• Performance Evaluation: 20% (Music use and Body Control – 0 to 10 points each)

• Major Deductions (Same as Final)

**Freestyle Judging Summary for 2016:**

**JUDGING GROUP A**

Technical Execution: 60%

• Two clickers (positive and negative). Normalized to 60 points maximum.

• Only technical aspect (difficulty, transitions, variation, risk, etc.)

• No additional points for rareness, cleanliness, style, continuity, etc.

• Technical execution judges will be very strict with repeating same tricks and/or elements

• Minus 1 for each missed string hit, missed trick, loss of control, missed bind, etc.

• Restarts, change outs, and other problems will be subject for deduction later (Major Deduction).

## JUDGING GROUP B

### Technical Evaluation: 20%

4 items: 0-5 points each. Not normalized. 20 points possible.

1. Cleanliness (Line of string, trajectory of yo-yo, smooth landings and transitions)

2. Variation (Different techniques within the style of play)

3. Rareness (Uniqueness, originality, difference within the contest framework)

4. Execution (No misses, perfection, completion, accuracy, precision)

Performance Evaluation: 30%

4 items: 0-5 points each. Not normalized. 20 points possible.

1. Music Use (Music timing, cueing, choreography, rhythm, imagery)

2. Space Use (Largeness, amplitude/focus, stage use)

3. Showmanship (theme/story, enjoyment, entertainment, overall impression of show)

4. Body Control (stage manners, posture, professionalism, attitude)

**Major Deductions:**

After totals of the Execution and Evaluation scores:

• 1 point deduction: Restart the spin on the yo-yo

• 3 point deduction: Change out the yo-yo for another one (any reason)

• 5 point deduction: Yo-Yo leaves stage, broken string, or mechanical failure

• Disqualification: Yo-Yo leaves front of stage and goes into the audience

# NINE

# GUIDE TO BUYING A YO-YO FOR YOUR TRICKS

SO YOU HAVE ALL these great yo-yo tricks up your sleeve but you want to update your yo-yo collection to make sure you have the best tricks for the trade. You do not need to feel overwhelmed with the various options available and even then, you should keep in mind that the player makes the yo-yo and not the other way around.

Any skilled yo-yo player has the ability to take any yo-yo they can find and perform tricks that would fill any audience with awe and amazement. Practice is the key element here because yo-yoing is just like any other skill out there and working at it is the only way you can genuinely improve your skills.

## Shapes

Yo-yos come in 3 basic shapes with the first one being as classic as they come. The Classic yo-yo shape is what would first come to people's minds when they imagine what a yo-yo looks like. It is the standard wooden yo-yo shape from when the instrument was initially introduced in the US and the shape is all-purpose making it awesome for all the classical yo-yo tricks.

If you are familiar with a yo-yo's appearance or its usage, then you have probably come across the wing-shaped or Flared Gap Shape yo-yos. This shape gives it a wide and V-shaped space making it much easier to catch your yo-yo back for tricks such as the Split the Atom or the Trapeze.

You could say this shape is the most dominant in the high-end and the metal yo-yo market. Why is that? This is because some of the most favored yo-yo tricks currently are the types where one catches their yo-yo while spinning on the string- also known as string tricks. However, if you are skilled at yo-yoing, you will be quite adept at doing such string tricks on yo-yos without a flared gap.

The Modified Shape yo-yos comprise most of the advanced yo-yos that have been brought in within the last 15 years. The shape is more streamlined compared to the Classic Shape. This makes it an ideal option for longer spin times and looping tricks.

The concept backing Modified Shape yo-yos was the development of a yo-yo possessing the benefits of the Classic and Flared Gap shapes. Modified shape yo-yos are smaller than Flared Gap yo-yos this makes them excellent for tighter Rock the Cradle Tricks and they have inside walls that are more rounded providing a wider gap.

This makes it easier to perform string tricks such as the Trapeze much easier compared to using the Classic Shape yo-yo but not more than the Flared Gap yo-yo. These types enable you to perform looping tricks better compared to flared gap yo-yos and as such, if you must only have one yo-yo type then it is the best choice.

## Types of Axles

The yo-yo axle is the point at which the yo-yo and the string connect and it also plays a role of holding together the two halves of the yo-yo. Various kinds of yo-yo axles exist each with its own benefits and features.

## Fixed yo-yos

The wooden axle was the pioneer when there was only one yo-yo type. Typically, yo-yos were carved out of a piece of solid wood meaning that the entire instrument was made from wood. Currently, wooden yo-yos are still available and they have maintained popularity due to their vintage 1950s feel.

A wooden axle yo-yo is an excellent, fun, and antici-pated option if you are looking to learn all the classic yo-yo tricks such as Rock the Baby, Around the World, or Walk the Dog. A wooden axle yo-yo is a great start if you played with one as a child and you are looking to use it again because they offer a sense of familiarity. There are fixed axle yo-yos with metal axles as well.

**Transaxle yo-yos**

These are yo-yos with a fixed axle and a sleeve around them that turns without any restriction. The sleeve enables longer spin time for the yo-yo in comparison to one with a basic fixed axle as it restricts friction whenever the yo-yo spins. The yo-yo sleeve can be metallic or plastic.

**Ball Bearing Axle Yo-yos**

These types spin even better than transaxle yo-yos do even though they are almost similar. The difference is that the sleeve is literally a metal device with tiny metal balls within it. Usually, the device itself is normally known as the bearing. The ball bearing axle has transformed the skill of yo-yoing by enabling longer spin times in comparison to preceding yo-yo types.

**Clutch Axle Yo-yos**

This kind makes use of centrifugal force to automatically awaken the yo-yo and come back to the user's hand. Centrifugal force keeps the clutch open when the instrument is spinning very fast. However, when the yo-yo's speed reduces, the clutch closes back up grabbing the axle, which in turn awakens the yo-yo again.

The clutch yo-yo is a good choice for anyone who is still green at yo-yoing and wishes to get to know the fundamentals. They are also ideal for people who are looking to learn a couple of standard yo-yo tricks but a majority of people move on from the clutch axle yo-yo to any of the other kinds.

**Unresponsive/ Non-responsive Ball Bearing Axle Yo-yo**

The hottest new trend is a yo-yo which does not wake up when you tug on its string after throwing a sleeper. For an unresponsive ball-bearing yo-yo to wake up one has to perform a special type of trick known as a bind. This will bunch the string up in a spinning yo-yo's gap and force the string to catch which makes the yo-yo climb up back into the user's hand.

The reason these yo-yos are trending is that they enable the user to perform a new variety of yo-yo tricks that cannot be done with the conventionally responsive yo-yo. Usually, unresponsive yo-yos are not ideal if you are a beginner.

In order to grasp the concept of the bind to make the yo-yo wake up again, you will need to master the art of throwing the yo-yo first. Learning how to bind can take hours or days of continuous practice if you are not familiar with the skill. If you are buying a yo-yo for the first time, you should check the description to see whether the yo-yo is mentioned as unresponsive. However, if you have already gotten to the intermediate stage of yo-yoing, you might want to buy one and try it for yourself.

**Yo-yo Materials**

Yo-yos are typically made from three materials namely Metal, Plastic and Wood.

**Wood** was used as the original material for yo-yos and it is still being used to date. Wood has a great feel in the user's hands and also possesses an ageless look that anyone would immediately perceive as a yo-yo.

Performing tricks using a wooden yo-yo means that you will genuinely impress the audience for being authentic.

**Plastic** is what a good number of the yo-yos in the market are made of because it is easy to mold into any shape; it is also tough and inexpensive. These features make it the go-to choice for the manufacture of high-performance yo-yos. With a plastic yo-yo, you can be sure to get the most out of it in terms of performance, color, and shape not to mention they are cool and fun to use.

A majority of metal yo-yos are typically made from aluminum. **Metallic** yo-yos are usually more expensive compared to their wooden or plastic counterparts due to the high expense of making them into the yo-yo shape and the materials' cost. Based on the yo-yo's design, metallic ones are heavier meaning that they offer longer spin periods with the proper yo-yoist. If you want to make a lasting impression, a shiny metallic one will do just that. This is because they are rare and they perform well and look equally great. However, you should be careful when using a metal yo-yo so that you do not hit something, someone, or even yourself with it.

.   .   .

## The Yo-yo String

This part of the yo-yo is not as complicated as people may think. One can simply use any regular cotton type 8 yo-yo string and it will work ideally. People have been using this string ever since the yo-yo began gaining popularity and it continues to be the overall top-selling string type for yo-yo use.

Probably the only rule of thumb concerning yo-yo string would be that you have to replace the string because the string has a tendency to wear out. The wear and tear of your yo-yo string depend directly on your yo-yo usage; the string wears out faster if you use your yo-yo more often. In addition, if the yo-yo string looks worn or is dirty, you should not keep using it because it might break and hurt someone in the event that the yo-yo flies off.

The string is inexpensive meaning you should not have a hard time regularly replacing it. Slick 6 and 8 strings are blended (part polyester and part cotton) so they are more durable than whole cotton strings. Other also believe they offer better performance and yo-yo enthusiasts prefer this type. Polyester string also exists for yo-yos and it lasts longer than plain cotton strings with the advantage of having a smoother feel.

# TEN

# MAINTAINING YOUR YO-YO FOR A BETTER PERFORMANCE

IF YOUR YO-YO is in good condition continuously, then your yo-yo will be in excellent spinning condition throughout.

**Stringing the Yo-yo**

Based on the type of yo-yo-you are using, you will need to place one to three loops around the axle. If you want to string your yo-yo, you should never take it apart to do so. The string will get caught in the axle and it could end up cutting in the axle threading when you are trying to screw it back on. A yo-yo string is merely a single long string that has been twisted up and folded in half. In order to string a yo-yo, take out the old string and untwist it until you are able to slip out the yo-yo.

To place one loop on the yo-yo, untwist your new

string at the end without a knot, which should be the bottom, to open up a large enough loop allowing you to slip it over the yo-yo and into the yo-yo string gap. Keep tension on the string while allowing it to retwist so as to avoid any kinks and you will be done.

To place two loops on the yo-yo, begin with a single loop but keep holding open the string after slipping it into the gap. Give the string half a twist and slip it over the yo-yo once more. For 3 loops, give it an additional half twist and slip it again over the yo-yo. After installing the right number of loops, you can retest the string again.

## Guidelines for Stringing a Yo-yo

This will give you a general idea of how many loops to put on the yo-yo. If you are not sure, begin with a single loop and add loops until the yo-yo comes back and sleeps easily.

The recommended number of loops for fixed axle yo-yos is one though some people prefer two for looping. For children, three is advisable so that the yo-yo does not sleep. This makes it easier for the yo-yo to get back into your hand.

Three loops are advisable for nylon transaxle yo-yos but if you are an advanced player, two loops will work just fine. One loop or two loops will work for yo-yos with a roller bearing. Typically one loop works best for adjustable string gap yo-yos but some people use two.

## Trimming the String to Make a Slipknot

For loop tricks, the string needs to be waist high to navel high on the player. If you find that the string is too long, you can cut it to about 4 inches above your waist and then tie a knot adjacent to the cut end.

## Placement of the String

A majority of the yo-yo players wear the yo-yo string on the middle finger between the first knuckle and the second one. This placement offers the best combination in terms of balance for better control when performing tricks and leverage for the performance of powerful throws.

## Winding up the String

For most beginners, winding the string can be a difficult task particularly for the roller bearing and transaxle yo-yos. The easiest way to do it is to put the index finger over the yo-yo string gap and wind it over the finger once. Afterwards, you will wind the string around twice again inside the string gap and under your finger. You will then slip the finger out and complete winding the yo-yo.

## Oiling

Yo-yos such as fireballs and brains with nylon transaxles need lubrication when they are making a screeching noise or if they are hard to get back into your hand. In order to oil the yo-yo, unscrew the transaxle and remove it. Put one drop of Teflon oil on the metal axle but on the smooth part. While doing this, you should make sure you avoid getting any oil on the axle threading. If there is oil on the threading then the yo-yo will not keep intact. Screw the yo-yo back in place after replacing the transaxle while taking great care not to over tighten it as this could result in damage.

It is rare for a roller bearing yo-yo to require any lubrication if at all because some of them, like Bumblebees, make use of sealed bearings. However, in the event that you feel the bearing requires some lubrication, then a tiny drop of Teflon oil placed on the side of the bearing in the groove will work just fine. As you play normally with the yo-yo, the oil will work its way into the bearing.

## Troubleshooting and Repair of Your Yo-yo

A yo-yo is just like any other mechanical object, which means that they are prone to occasional problems. You should be prepared in case there is any such problem with your yo-yo so that you can fix it quickly and get it back into tip-top shape.

**1.** If you need to take the axle out without damaging or scratching it, you will have better luck wrapping around the axle with a heavy rubber band or something similar. This will protect the axle before unscrewing it from the yo-yo using pliers.

**2.** In the event that your cap falls off, which normally happens when the yo-yo hits too hard on the ground, you can use some super glue to put it back on.

**3.** New yo-yos usually have a knob or a mold mark present on the edge and this should not alarm you in any way.

**4.** The yo-yo will not come apart: Yo-yos with a fixed axle and most wooden yo-yos have not been designed to come apart. You can remove string tangles carefully using a paper clip but you should make sure you do not scratch the axle or the inside of your yo-yo. If the yo-yo is cracked or stripped, it might not come apart. When screwing the yo-yo back together take care not to use excessive force and make sure you trim the string making sure that you do not hit the ground to keep something like that from happening.

**5.** The yo-yo refuses to screw back together or it keeps dismantling- With time, it is completely normal for a take-apart yo-yo to work its way apart, which is why you should check it for tightness during usage. Wipe off any oil from the threading of the axle and screw it back together until it is tight enough, make sure you do not crack the plastic areas or strip off the threading. If the nut or the threading is stripped or if the plastic surrounding the nut is cracked, then the yo-yo might not stay together or screw back together. When screwing it back on, use less force and trim the string to avoid hitting the ground.

**6.** The yo-yo string keeps breaking: it is not uncommon for a yo-yo string to break especially after a maximum of 8 hours of play. This could be less for advanced players who are using wooden axle yo-yos. A red flag would be if the string breaks after just a few minutes of play on a fixed axle yo-yo. This could mean that the axle is possibly scratched and this could cut through the string very fast. The string might be caught in the threading of the axle (take-apart yo-yos). The string will cut very fast if it falls off a bearing. Check to make sure all the parts within the yo-yo are in the right order and if it has an adjustable gap this might have been widened beyond the bearing's width.

7. The yo-yo will not come back (fixed-axle): Just twist the string in such a way that it is tighter around the

yo-yo's axle. Another option would be to replace a thin, old string with a fluffy, new string.

**8.** The Brain will not automatically come back: ensure the string is twisted tightly and triple looped around the yo-yo transaxle to make sure it does not slip. The O-ring also wears down following enough use from the clutch closing around it. If the O-ring appears flat instead of rounded on the edges, then it needs replacement. Wipe off any oil from the clutch and the O-ring. The clutch could also be broken in a way that it cannot close on the O-ring tightly. This happens when the yo-yo hits hard on the ground.

**9.** The yo-yo will not sleep: First, ensure the string is looped around the axle and not tied. Search for any knots in the string or untwist it slightly to allow free spinning of the axle within the loop. Remove tangled string from a non-take-apart yo-yo using a metallic or sharp object such as a pair of scissors or a paper clip.

# ELEVEN

# MAKING MONEY WITH YOUR YO-YO TRICKS

SOME PEOPLE MIGHT BE LOOKING to make yo-yoing into a career while some just view it as a fun hobby introducing you to a new social group and tapping into new skills. However, you might not be able to make sufficient money to make a living off it but you can make enough to help you pay for competitions or buy some new yo-yos. Here are some of the ways in which you can do that.

## Sell Beginner Yo-Yos

Some people attest to this method working fairly well for them. There are festivals and farmers markets in various cities with the need for children's entertainers. You can offer to provide free entertainment in exchange for selling yo-yos. You can buy decent yo-yos at good wholesale prices and sell them at a profit especially if you are selling them with website links, a card, and some extra string. You can paint them to give them additional value. Perform some of the simpler tricks to capture people's attention and then offer them a chance to try it. Teach them the basic moves especially children then suggest to the parent that they can also try it.

**Performing**

A few professional yo-yoers make a living performing and they perform simple tricks with a bit of drama, some jokes and plenty of smiles. As a Yo-yoer, walking the dog is the best trick to learn aside from two-handed loop tricks if you are looking to perform. It might be hard to find paying gigs but they exist.

**The Internet**

The yo-yo market is huge out there and more people are looking to get involved. As long as your content is genuinely original and you can garner 1000 daily views, YouTube can pay you. You can make tutorials and use your own music so you gain all the ad revenue and the credit. You can make some good money if you work to ensure your videos reach a bigger audience.

## Birthdays and Children's Workshops

This can be tricky but it works well for some people particularly if you have the necessary skills to handle a group of children to teach them the skill of yo-yoing. However, it needs patience to do this and the ability to shift your focus to a group without dedicating too much time to a single person showing excitement.

## Street Performances

You need the heart to do street performances because when starting out the money will have you thinking that it is not worth it. Select a few tricks that you can perform without thinking twice and figure out how to engage with people. If you do not tell people that they should pay you, then they will not. Greet people and offer to allow them to try a yo-yo trick. Simpler tricks resonate with people. Before going into Yo-yo Street performing, ensure you check on local by-laws concerning street performing and ensure you have a small area to capture people's attention further.

The suggestions all share the concept of teaching and performance. Performance needs one to master the basic skills and have the ability to charm and interact with an audience.

# TWELVE
## ADDITIONAL TRICKS

### 43. **Fake Binds**

This trick is all about different ways to pull your yo-yo back to your hand.

### 44. Binding

When your yo-yo does not respond to the normal tug, this trick works best.

Yo-yos with very little response can usually only be recalled to your hand with what is known as a Bind.

To wake up such a yo-yo, you have to more or less take care of creating more response yourself. You can do this by increasing the number of strings for the axle to catch onto.

The Bind works as follows:

**Step One:** Start with a Trapeze or an Under Mount and pull the loop made by this trick over the yo-yo.

**Step Two:** The additional loop now wraps more string around the axle so that by drawing the loop into the string gap, you can recall an unresponsive yo-yo to your hand. This also works when the yo-yo is spinning in the opposite direction (Backspin Bind).

## 45. Flying Saucer

This refers to a throw that is done sideways to loosen or tighten the string.

**Step One:** Throw the yo-yo diagonally at a 45 degree angle downwards to the left (as a right hander). If you throw it flat enough, you can let it sleep horizontally to perform a UFO.

**Step Two**: Grip the string approximately 20 cm above the yo-yo and lift the yo-yo upwards so that it keeps rotating on its side.

**Step Three:** With a short tug of your free hand you can recall the yo-yo to your throw hand. This trick quickly unravels twisted strings and adjusts string tension. Throwing a UFO to the right tightens up the string.

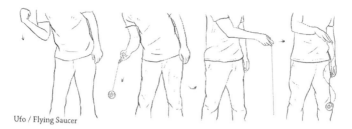

Ufo / Flying Saucer

*Tip: A yo-yo with more response is helpful for this trick.*

**String Tricks**

**46. Barrel Rolls.**

The trick has similarities with the forward and reverses flips, and it can be performed from both the front-mount and side-mount.

**Step one**: Start with the front-mount approach.

**Step two**: Take the first finger on your yoyo hand (based on your suitability), and stick it between the two strings.

**Step three**: Swing the yoyo slowly, and try to hop it over your finger.

**Step four**: Take the first finger on the opposite hand, and quickly pull that corresponding finger just right under your yoyo. That's the first revolution of the barrel rolls.

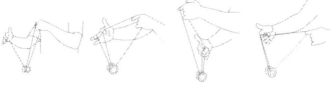

Barrel Rolls

*Tip: If you want to go for the side-mount trick, you simply need to follow the reverse direction. Place the yoyo on its string, and stick your finger between those strings (don't push forward, as you want to roll reverse). It's fun and easy.*

## 47. Kwijibo

This is one of the hardest tricks and it consists of many hoops.

**Step One**: Start with a Trapeze.

**Step Two**: Pop the yo-yo up in the air, cross your arms (right over left) and catch the yo-yo on the front string.

**Step Three**: Now cross your arms in the other direction (left over right), pop the yo-yo once more into the air and catch it in a Double or Nothing.

**Step Four**: Finish off as for a Double or Nothing.

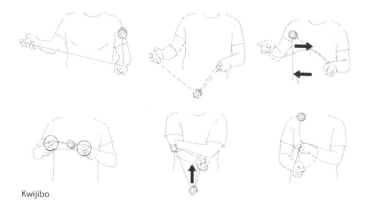

Kwijibo

## 48. Triangle Symmetry

This trick is common for freestyles.

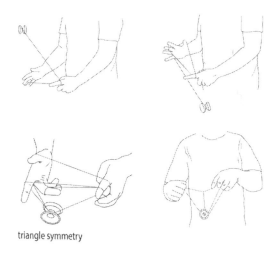

triangle symmetry

## 49. Green Triangle

A green triangle trick is like you reach a destination, for example, from your school to home. In this case, your yoyo will be in your place. What I actually meant that you would see different tricks which may end up in different ways, but in this case, it won't if you can do it properly.

**Step One**: Go behind the string and place it over your preferred hand. The preferred hand means whether you prefer right hand or left hand.

**Step Two**: Let the rest of the string fall off your hand. In order to create a green triangle, you should pop the yoyo out towards you, and then the opposite, as shown in the picture. After that pop the yoyo up.

green triangle

## 50. Folds

Fold means folding something, like a piece of paper or clothes. You can do a folding trick with the yoyo as well. The instructions are as the following:

**Step One**: Do a trapeze. It's like making a loop around one of your thumbs, and pull the string with another hand.

**Step Two**: Pull the loop a bit upward with your free hand.

**Step Three**: Try folding it over your hand. The hand which you will use to throw the yoyo.

**Step Four**: You will see your throw hand is getting stuck around the strings. So you need to release your throw hand from the strings.

**Step Five**: Start hanging the yoyo in the loop. Slowly place your thumb of the throwing hand inside the loop you just created.

**Step Six**: Pull the throw hand thumb a little bit wide. Pop the yoyo up and forward. Make sure your free hand's index finger and the thumb inside the loop.

**Step Seven**: You will see a twisted string. Start the pinwheel, and move in front.

**Step Eight**: The yoyo will keep operating around your freehand index finger. Land the strings between your throw thumb and the index finger of your free hand.

**Step Nine**: Involve more fingers into the loop of the yoyo and quickly pull out your index finger.

**Step Ten**: You can now drop the loop around the thumb of your throw hand.

Following those ten steps, you can repeat as much time as you want. Give it a try!

## 51. Chop Sticks

This refers to when string tricks are done on one hand between the fingers.

## 52. Spirit Bomb

This trick is perfect when combined with the wrist mount.

**Step One**: Start with the wrist mount.

**Step Two**: Try creating the loop around your wrist, as shown in the illustration.

**Step Three**: Roll under the yoyo, instead of twisting your hand. You are going to roll your yoyo under those two strings in the photo. Once you get the rhythm, you will see the yoyo is rolling at itself, without you putting much effort.

**Step Four**: Toss the yoyo up while it is rolling. You will notice a bit of triangle up there, with a string below it. Land the yoyo on that string.

**Step Five**: Roll back, and twist your hand. While you roll back, the string will be at your closest distance. You can now quickly get the yoyo back to your hand.

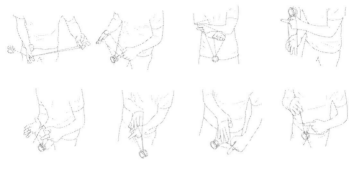

Spirit bomb

*Tip: The trickiest part is the step three where you have to uncross your hand from the two strings. So practicing more will make you an expert.*

### 53. Tsunami Bomb

The Tsunami bomb is one of the funniest tricks. Follow the tricks:

**Step One**: Start with 1.5 mount, and determine your throw hand thumb. Put the throw hand thumb under the top string as described in the photo.

**Step Two**: See the photo described. Use the index

fingertip of your free hand, and thumb of your throw hand.

**Step Three**: Underpass the string over your tip finger.

**Step Four**: Take the bottom three fingers with the throwing hand and stick them out of the string leading directly down. Now you will have four fingers occupied where your yoyo is located.

**Step Five**: Swing the yoyo over the top toward your throw hand side, and land on the string where the yoyo is located.

**Step Six**: The yoyo will go over your hand and land back on the string.

**Step Seven**: Take the opposite point finger out of the string mess. From here, take the opposite hand pointer finger underpassing the yoyo.

**Step Eight**: Take your opposite hand thumb and hook it under the string coming from your throw hand thumb.

**Step Nine**: Pass the yoyo over the top of the throw thumb just like a chopstick.

**Step Ten**: Hop the yoyo straight up through the triangle you formed, and land the yoyo back into a trapeze.

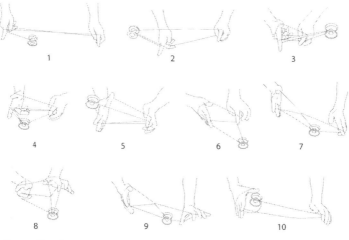

Tsunami bomb

**Note**: *The trickiest part is step three where you have to uncross your hand from the two strings. So practicing more will make you an expert.*

## 54. Eli Hops

This is one of the most engaging and visually pleasing tricks.

**Step One**: Start with a Trapeze.

**Step Two**: Pop the yo-yo up above your head while at the same time widening and narrowing the distance between your hands on the string.

**Step Three**: Land the yo-yo onto the string. This

impressive trick can be repeated as often as you like. A yo-yo with less response is helpful for this trick.

## 55. McBride's Coaster

**Step One**: Starts with a breakaway (see breakaway pag.36) it is called the world tour it's around the world but sideways.

**Step Two**: So breakaway once around and then we're going into the one and a half mount.

**Step Three**: Then we are going to swing out of a one and a half mount completely around back to trapeze and his brother to swing around to double or nothing (see double or nothing pag.115)

**Step Four**: Then we drop off here, we are going to do a roll, we put a finger in the triangle already formed and then we swing it twice.

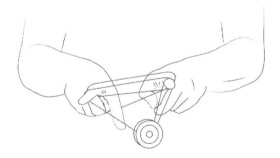

McBride's Coaster

## 56. Mag Rolls

This is one of the easiest and most fun tricks to be done.

## 57. Lindy Loop

This is a trapeze closely followed by another trapeze.

**Step One**: Throw a Trapeze but swing the string twice around over your finger. Can you do this even more often?

## 58. Man On The Flying Trapeze And His Brother

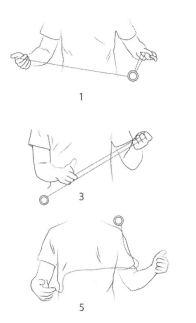

1

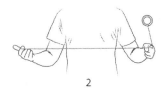

2

3

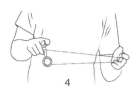

4

5

Man On The Flying Trapeze And His Brother

## 59. Boingy Boing

Split bottom mount rhythmic trick.

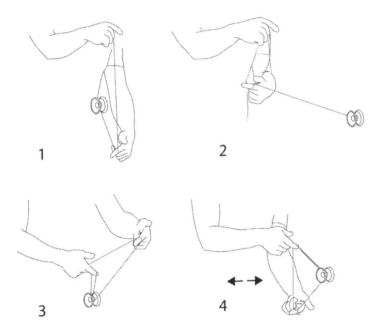

## 60. Pop N Fresh

This is a split bottom with multiple pops as the name suggests.

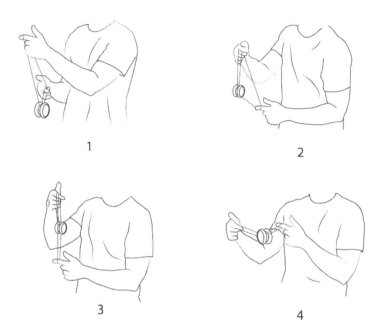

1

2

3

4

Pop and fresh

## 61. Mach 5

This is a split bottom mount trick where your hands are spinning and the yo-yo seems to be floating.

## 62. Atom Smasher

This refers to a Split bottom mount with underpasses and tosses.

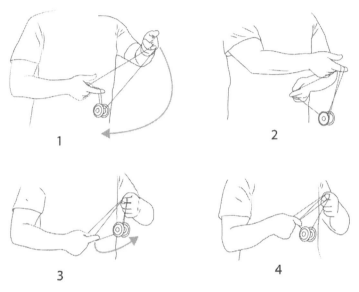

Atom smasher

## 63. Split The Atom

This trick is a brain twister with an extra underpass.

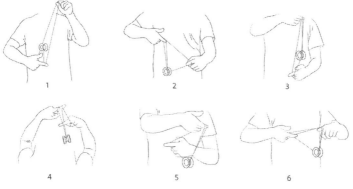

Split the Atom

## 64. Barrel Rolls

This trick has infinite underpasses.

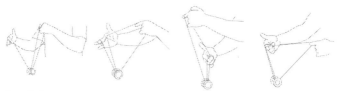

Barrel Rolls

## 65. Brain Twister

To perform the under mount, this trick is a must.

**Step One:** Start with a hard Sleeper.

**Step Two:** Push the index finger of your free hand forward into the string.

**Step Three:** Run it up the string until it is approximately 1/3 of the string length above the yo-yo. At the same time, move the throw hand holding the end of the string underneath the yo-yo and then bring it upwards.

**Step Four:** Push the string with the index finger of your throw hand and swing the yo-yo forwards. (With a little practice, you can repeat the loop as often as you like.)

**Step Five:** To finish off the trick, flip the yo-yo off the string and wake it up.

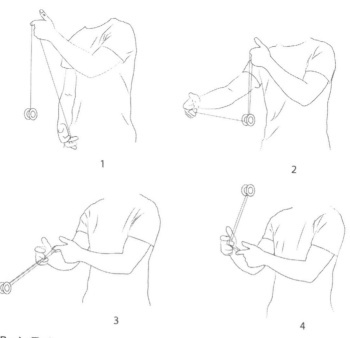

Brain Twister

## 66. Over And Under

This trick combines two mounts.

## 67. Over Mount

This trick is the opposite of the under mount.

## 68. Under Mount

This trick is simply a front style mount.

Throw a Sleeper and use the momentum of the yo-yo to swing it round to land directly on the string again.

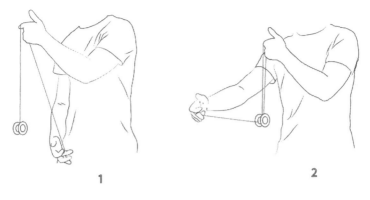

1                                    2

Under Mount

## 69. Reverse Trapeze

This is similar to the trapeze but the opposite of the trick.

## 70. Double or Nothing

This trick is a breakaway that goes around twice before landing on the left finger trapeze style.

**Step One**: Start as you would for a Trapeze with a Breakaway and swing the yo-yo over the index finger of your free hand. However, the distance between your hands is shorter for the Double or Nothing.

**Step Two**: Position the index finger of your throw hand and swing the yo-yo around it.

**Step Three**: Now the yo-yo must loop around the

index finger of the other hand and land on the front string.

**Step Four:** To dismount you can let all the strings drop again or finish the Double or Nothing with a windmill. To do this, simply drop the string from the index finger of your throw hand and swing the yo-yo outwards over the other hand twice.

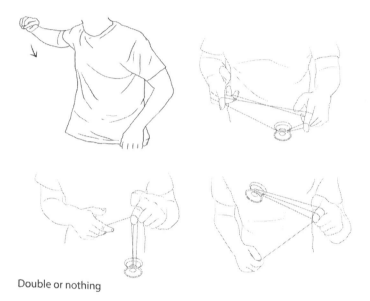

Double or nothing

## 71. Man on the Flying Trapeze

**Step One**: Start with a Breakaway to the right.

**Step Two**: When the yo-yo has swung back to the left

in front of your body, extend the index finger of your free hand and catch the string on it near to the yo-yo.

**Step Three**: When the string and the yo-yo swing around the index finger, try to catch the yo-yo on the long part of the string.

## Grinds

### 72. Thumb Grind.

In this trick, First start with a trapeze and the thumb is used as the yo-yo ring.

Thumb Grind

### 73. Finger Grind

For this trick, grind the yo-yo with your yo-yo finger.

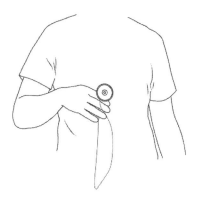

Finger Grind

## 74. Arm Grind

This trick is all about grinding your yo-yo on your hand.

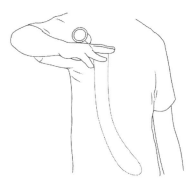

Arm Grind

## 75. Inner Ring Grind

For this trick, the yo-yo hangs on your finger tip.

## Inner Finger Ring

**Slack String Tricks**

## 76. Wave slack.

This trick is a cool slack.

## 77. Iron whip

This is a very hard whip.

**Step One:** Throw a Trapeze.

**Step Two:** Grip the string leading to the yo-yo below the index finger of your free hand with the index, middle and ring fingers of the throw hand.

**Step Three:** Remove your index finger from the Trapeze while swinging the complete loop backwards and then whip it around the yo-yo. For this trick, the momentum must come from the wrist. To add more Iron Whips, simply use the index finger and start again from the beginning.

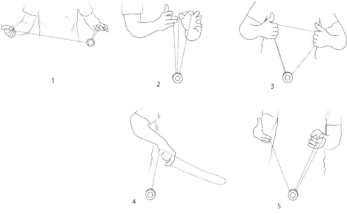

Iron Whip

## 78. Plastic Whip

This trick is a one handed slack mount.

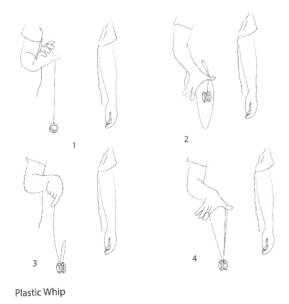

Plastic Whip

## 79. Hidemasa Hook

This is an improvement to the reverse slack trapeze.

Hidemasa or Hook

## 80. Slack trapeze

This is a simplified whip for the trapeze.

Slack Trapeze

## 81. **Reverse Slack Trapeze**

This trick is the reverse of the slack trapeze.

### Two handed play

For this play, two yo-yos are involved. Each yo-yo is attached to a specific hand.

### Counterweight

Free hand. For this play, the yo-yo is tied to a counter-weight which could be a rubber ball or die as opposed to being tied to your throw hand.

### Off string

## 82. **Open String Whip**

This is one of the hardest but coolest tricks to learn.

Open string Whip

## 83. Off String Whip

This is one of the most cool-looking off string tricks.

## 84. Off String Basics

This is the basic trick to learn when it comes to off string tricks.

### Exotic Stuff

## 85. Flytrap

This trick is cross genre where the aim is to catch the open slipknot loop back to the fingers.

## 86. Invisi-whip

For this play, it is very similar to the Skyrocket trick. It involves directly working the slipknot to mount in the air and bring back the hand.

## 87. Moebicide Suicide

For this trick, maneuver with your yoyo is in the slip-knot loop.

## 88. Hoophia

With this trick, this yoyo spins around in the slipknot in an infinite loop.

## 89. Ghost rider

For this play, the yoyo is put in a sleeping position and held there. The notch around your finger is then taken off and held by your thumb and index finger.

## 90. Washing Machine

This play involves untying the loop that goes on the yo-yo to do off string style tricks.

### Step 1:

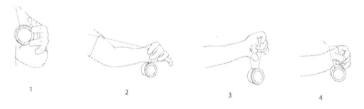

Washing Machine

### Step 2:

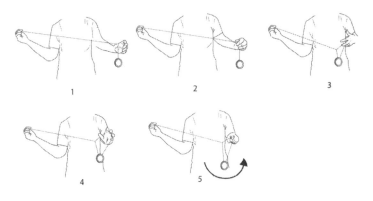

Washing Machine

## Other Tricks to Have a Look At

There are some additional tricks which we will not look into in too much detail. These consist mostly of freestyles and include the following:

### 91. Wind the String

Wind the String

### 92. Flips

### 93. String trick / ripcord

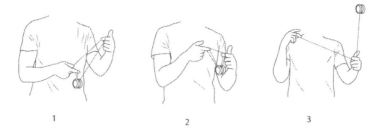

1        2        3

Ripcord  String Trick

## 94. **Side Mount Corrections**

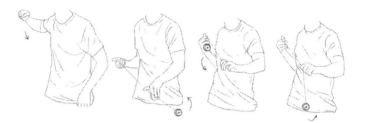

## 95. **Reverse Flip Front Mount**

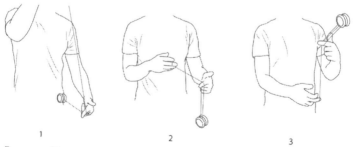

1        2        3

Reverse flip mount

## 96. Regenerations

While the yo-yo is spinning in a sleeper, it is accelerated outwards and dropped into a fast sleeper.

**Step One**: First of all you wake up the yo-yo.

**Step Two**: However, you don't catch it directly with your hand but quickly snap it back into a sleeper again. This allows you to perform long, fluid combos without catching the yo-yo

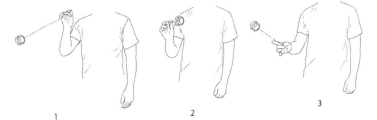

Regenerations

## 97. Snap Wind

Snap Wind

## 98. **Binds**

## 99. **Split Bottom Mount**

1         2         3

4         5

Split Bottom Mount Yoyo Trick

## 100. Man on The Flying Trapeze and His Brother Slack

1     2     3

Man on the flying trapeze and his brother slack

## 101. Buddha's Revenge

1     2

3     4

Buddha's revenge

# AFTERWORD

I hope this book was able to help you to get started on your journey to becoming an expert yo-yoer.

Yo-yoing is a fun skill to learn not to mention it can introduce you to an entirely new audience or crowd and it will push you to expand your horizons in a way.

However, yo-yo tricks require a lot of practice and you need to dedicate adequate time and energy to it if you want to perfect the skill. There are also several levels to it so you can perform the tricks at your skill level and if you are proficient, you can participate in competitions worldwide or simply share your skills with others.

I hope through this book you have mastered the art of doing tricks with your yo-yo starting from beginner tricks to intermediate and finally, expert tricks. I also hope that you have seen the possibilities of the yo-yo well beyond it being just another toy. Remember, you can make money and win world contents just based off your tricks.

Take time to practice these tricks and even invent more if you can! As mentioned before, patience is key when it comes to this therefore, take time to do a bit of research and even watch some videos online for additional information.

All the best on your journey to expert yo-yoing!

Good luck!